Abbreviations and Symbols

beg . . . . begin(ning)
BL(s) . . . . back loop(s)
ch(s) . . . . chain(s)
dc . . . . double crochet(s)
dec . . . . decrease(-ing)
FL(s) . . . . front loop(s)
FPdc . . . . front post double crochet(s)
gm(s) . . . . gram(s)
hdc . . . . half double crochet(s)
lp(s) . . . . loop(s)
oz . . . . ounce(s)
patt . . . . pattern
prev . . . . previous
rem . . . . remain(ing)
rep . . . . repeat(ing)
rnd(s) . . . . round(s)
sc . . . . single crochet(s)
sk . . . . skip
sl . . . . slip
sl st(s) . . . . slip stitch(es)
sp(s) . . . . space(s)
st(s) . . . . stitch(es)
tog . . . . together
yd(s) . . . . yard(s)
YO . . . . yarn over

* An asterisk is used to mark the beginning of a portion of instructions to be worked more than once; thus, "rep from ***** twice more" means after working the instructions once, repeat the instructions following the asterisk twice more (3 times in all).

† The dagger identifies a portion of instructions that will be repeated again later in the same row or round.

— The number after a long dash at the end of a row or round indicates the number of stitches you should have when the row or round has been completed. The long dash can also be used to indicate a completed stitch such as a decrease or a shell.

() Parentheses are used to enclose instructions which should be worked the exact number of times specified immediately following the parentheses, such as "(2 sc in next dc, sc in next dc) twice." They are also used to set off and clarify a group of stitches that are to be worked all into the same space or stitch, such as "(2 dc, ch 1, 2 dc) in corner sp."

[] Brackets and **()** parentheses are used to provide additional information to clarify instructions.

Join - join with a sl st unless otherwise specified.

The patterns in this book are written using United States terminology. Terms which have different English equivalents are noted below.

United States	English
single crochet (sc)	double crochet (dc)
half double crochet (hdc)	half treble (htr)
double crochet (dc)	treble (tr)
skip (sk)	miss
slip stitch (sl st)	slip stitch (ss) or "single crochet"
gauge	tension
yarn over (YO)	yarn over hook (YOH)

Terms

Front loop (abbreviated FL) is the loop toward you at the top of the stitch (**Fig 1**).

Back loop (abbreviated BL) is the loop away from you at the top of the stitch (**Fig 1**).

Post is the vertical part of the stitch (**Fig 1**).

Wrong side: Wrong side of the work—the side that will not show when project is in use.

Right side: The side that will show.

Right-hand side: The side nearest your right hand as you are working.

Left-hand side: The side nearest your left hand as you are working.

Evenly spaced: The stitches are to be spaced at an even distance from each other.

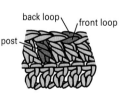

back loop front loop
post

Fig 1

Lots of Socks

Crocheted socks?

Sure, why not?

This collection is both fun and functional. The socks are great to wear and wonderful, quick to make gifts. We've done them in two weights, worsted and sport and included a design to wear with clogs.

Have fun using bright colors, or stick to the pastels or neutrals. Get out your hook and you'll soon have the fanciest feet in town!

Crocheting Socks

About the Yarn

Ideally, yarn used for socks should have some wool content, which makes them more absorbent. Acrylic yarns, however, are more readily available, so that is what we used.

Worsted Weight Yarns

Try to use the new "soft" worsted weight yarns, as they will mold to the foot well and be more comfortable. If using regular worsted acrylic, you may want to wash the socks with fabric softener before wearing or giving.

Our worsted weight socks are worked to a gauge of 4 sc = 1".

Sport or DK Weight Yarns

These yarns make a nice, light sock. You'll see the term "DK weight" turning up more often on labels, as more yarns come in from outside the U.S. DK and sport are interchangeable in most cases, though the DK is sometimes a bit heavier. So be sure to check your gauge carefully.

Our sport/DK weight socks are worked to a gauge of 5 sc = 1".

About that Gauge

We know you cover your ears or turn up the TV when we mention gauge! Most crocheters hate having to worry about it, but if you want your socks to fit, you really do have to take the time to work a gauge swatch. Although our patterns give suggested hook sizes, you need to use whatever hook size it takes to get the stitch gauge. At least in socks, you don't have to worry about row gauge too!

Making Socks that Fit

A good fit is essential in socks. Because the acrylic yarns don't have the elasticity of those with wool content, we have given two sizes for each design—small (shoe size 6 to 8) and medium (shoe size 8½ to 10½). This sizing is based on an average ankle circumference of 8" for small and 9" for medium. For a thicker than average ankle, you may wish to use a larger size hook for the cuff ribbing and ankle portion only.

The length of the sole will differ from foot to foot—women come in a variety of shapes and sizes, and their feet can be long, short, wide or narrow. For a thinner than average foot, you may wish to use a smaller size hook for the foot and toe portion of the sock.

The best way to judge length is to have the person who is to wear the sock stand barefoot on a flat surface while you measure her foot length from back of heel to tip of the longest toe. If you can't measure an actual foot, ask the recipient-to-be for her shoe size.

These are the average measurements to use as a guide for sizing your socks from women's shoe sizes.

Guide to Shoe Sizes

Shoe Size	Foot Measurement	Sock Length
6-6½	9"	8¾"
7-7½	9⅜"	9"
8-8½	9¾"	9¼"
9-9½	10"	9¾"
10-10½	10⅜"	10"

Also, most of the socks in this book have been made using more than one color yarn. If you choose to make your socks all in one color, each pair requires approximately 4 to 6 oz of worsted weight yarn or sport/DK weight.

Anatomy of a Sock

We put them on almost every day, but we don't often examine socks to see how they are constructed. Our socks that are made with a heel, are worked from the cuff down (see **Fig 1**).

Fig 1

Cupped Heel Socks

Cuff:
This part is worked in a stretchy stitch which is designed to let you slip the sock on more easily.

Ankle:
This part is worked even in the round from the end of the cuff to the start of the heel flap and instep. Continuous rounds avoid the bulk of a seam.

Next the work is divided and the heel flap and cup-shaped heel turning are worked first.

Heel Flap:
This piece goes down the back of the heel up to where the heel cup begins to take shape and is worked in rows.

Heel Turning:
Because a heel is at an angle to the leg, socks must be shaped the same way. This is done by a series of decrease rows which turns the direction of the work and creates a sort of cup to enclose your heel. This is called "turning the heel."

Once the heel is turned, the work is rejoined and worked in rounds for the remainder of the sock.

Gusset:
For the gusset you pick up stitches on each side of the heel flap to change direction again, and rejoin it to the instep.

Foot:
Now the sock is worked in rounds until it measures 2½" less than the desired finished length of the work. This is where you can make adjustments for length of the foot. The foot is measured from the back edge of the heel.

Toe Shaping:
The last 2½" are used to shape the toe with a series of decreases. The last row leaves stitches which need to be sewn together in as smooth a manner as possible to provide comfort when wearing the sock.

Tube Sock

We have also included a tube sock—*Footloose*. This sock is made as a tube with no heel shaping. For this type of sock the crocheted fabric needs to be worked loosely so that the sock can form itself to the foot.

Tube socks usually begin at the toe, and end at the cuff. One advantage is that if you have no idea of the shoe size of the recipient, the tube sock will fit almost anyone!

The Learning Section

Lesson 1: Getting Started

To crochet socks, you need only a crochet hook, some yarn and a tapestry needle.

Yarn

Yarn comes in many sizes; from fine crochet cotton used for doilies, to wonderful bulky mohairs used for afghans and sweaters. The most commonly used yarn is a medium size, called worsted weight (sometimes called 4-ply). It is readily available in a wide variety of beautiful colors. This is the weight we will use in our lessons. Always read yarn labels carefully. The label will tell you how much yarn is in the skein or ball, in ounces, grams or yards; the type of yarn, its washability, and sometimes how to pull the yarn from the skein. Also, there is usually a dye lot number. This number assures you that the color of each skein with this number is the same. The same color may vary from dye lot to dye lot creating variations in color when a project is completed. Therefore, when purchasing yarn for a project, it is important to match the dye lot number on the skeins.

You'll need a blunt-pointed sewing needle with an eye big enough to carry the yarn for weaving in yarn ends and sewing seams. This is a size 16 steel tapestry needle.

Hooks

Crochet hooks, too come in many sizes, from very fine steel hooks used to make intricate doilies and lace, to great big fat ones of plastic or wood used to make bulky sweaters or rugs.

The hooks you will use for your socks are made of aluminum, are about 6" long, and are sized alphabetically by letter from B (the smallest) to K. For our lessons, you'll need a size H hook, a medium size.

The aluminum crochet hook looks like this:

In **Fig 2**, (**A**) is the hook end, which is used to hook the yarn and draw it through other loops of yarn (called stitches). (**B**) is the throat, a shaped area that helps you slide the stitch up onto (**C**) the working area. (**D**) is the fingerhold, a flattened area that helps you grip the hook comfortably, usually with your thumb and third finger; and (**E**) is the handle, which rests under your fourth and little fingers, and provides balance for easy, smooth work.

Fig 2

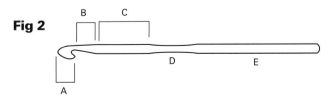

continued

Lesson 1: Getting Started *(continued)*

It is important that every stitch is made on the working area, never on the throat (which would make the stitch too tight) and never on the fingergrip (which would stretch the stitch).

The hook is held in the right hand, with the thumb and third finger on the fingergrip, and the index finger near the tip of the hook (**Fig 3**).

Fig 3

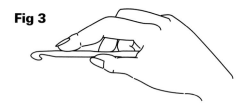

The hook should be turned slightly toward you, not facing up or down. **Fig 4** shows how the hook is held, viewing from underneath the hand. The hook should be held firmly, but not tightly.

Fig 4

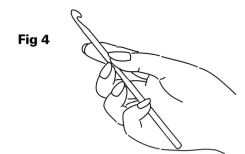

Lesson 2: Chain Stitch (abbreviated ch)

Crochet begins with a series of chain stitches called a beginning or starting chain. Begin by making a slip knot on the hook about 4" from the thread end. Loop the yarn as in **Fig 5**.

Fig 5

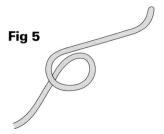

Insert hook through center of loop and hook the free end (**Fig 6**).

Fig 6

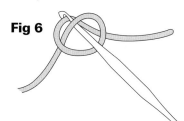

Pull this through and up onto the working area of the hook (**Fig 7**).

Fig 7

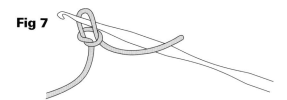

Pull yarn end to tighten the loop (**Fig 8**).

Fig 8

It should be firm, but loose enough to slide back and forth easily on the hook. Be sure you still have about a 4" yarn end.

Hold the hook, now with its slip knot, in your right hand (**Fig 9**).

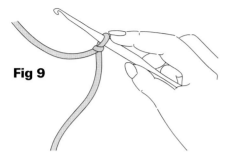

Fig 9

Now let's make the first chain stitch.

Step 1: Hold the base of the slip knot with the thumb and index finger of your left hand, and thread yarn from the ball over the middle finger (**Fig 10**)

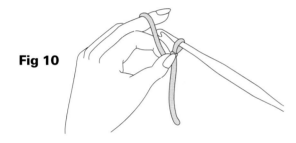

Fig 10

and under the remaining fingers of the left hand (**Fig 10a**).

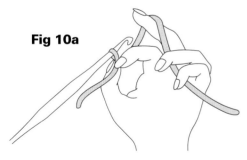

Fig 10a

Your middle finger will stick up a bit to help the thread feed smoothly from the ball; the other fingers help maintain even tension on the yarn as you work.

Hint: As you practice, you can adjust the way your left hand holds the yarn to whatever is most comfortable for you.

Step 2: Bring the yarn over the hook from back to front and hook it (**Fig 11**).

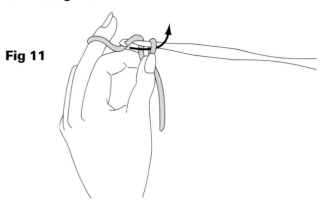

Fig 11

Draw hooked yarn through the loop of the slip knot on the hook and up onto the working area of the hook (see arrow on **Fig 11**); you have now made one chain stitch (**Fig 12**).

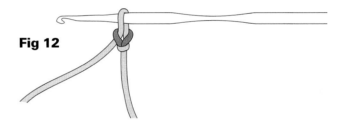

Fig 12

Step 3: Again bring the yarn over the hook from back to front (**Fig 13**).

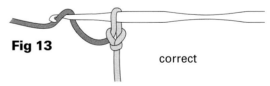

Fig 13

correct

Note: Take care not to bring yarn from front to back (**Fig 13a**).

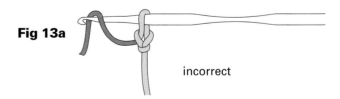

Fig 13a

incorrect

Hook it and draw through loop on the hook: you have made another chain stitch (**Fig 14**).

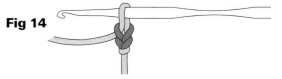

Fig 14

continued

Repeat Step 3 for each additional chain stitch, being careful to move the left thumb and index finger up the chain close to the hook after each new stitch or two (**Fig 15**). This helps you control the work. Also be sure to pull each new stitch up onto the working area of the hook.

Fig 15

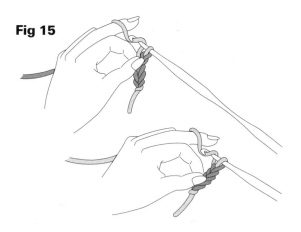

The working yarn and the work in progress are always held in your left hand.

Practice making chains until you are comfortable with your grip of the hook and the flow of the yarn; in the beginning your work will be uneven, with some chain stitches loose and others tight. While you're learning, try to keep the chain stitches loose. As your skill increases, the chain should be firm, but not tight, with all chain stitches even in size.

Hint: As you practice, if the hook slips out of a stitch, don't get upset! Just insert the hook again from the front into the center of the last stitch, taking care not to twist the loop (**Fig 16**).

Fig 16

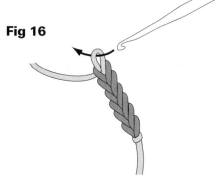

Chain stitches are also worked between other stitches to create open spaces.

Lesson 3: Working into the Chain

Once you have worked the beginning chain, you are ready to begin the stitches required to make a sock. These stitches are worked into the starting chain. For practice, make 6 chains loosely.

Hint: When counting your chain stitches at the start of a pattern – which you must do very carefully before continuing – note that the loop on the hook is never counted as a stitch; and the starting slip knot is never counted as a stitch (**Fig 17**).

Fig 17

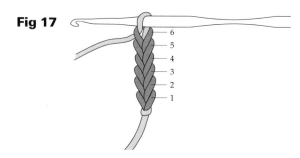

Now stop and look at the chain. The front looks like a series of interlocking V's (**Fig 17**), and each stitch has a bump or ridge at the back (**Fig 18**).

Fig 18

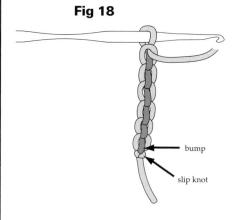

bump

slip knot

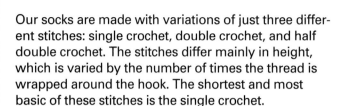

You will never work into the first chain from the hook. Depending on the stitch, you will work into the second, third, fourth, etc. chain from the hook. The instructions will always state how many chains to skip before starting the first stitch.

When working a stitch, insert hook from the front of the chain, through the center of a V stitch, and under the corresponding bump on the back of the same stitch (**Fig 19**).

Fig 19

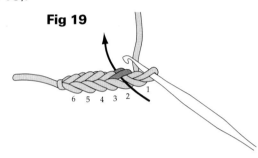

Excluding the first stitch, you will work into every stitch in the chain unless the pattern states differently, but not into the starting slip knot (**Fig 19a**). Be sure that you do not skip that last chain at the end.

Fig 19a

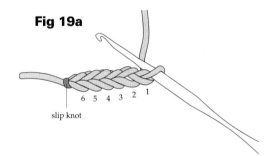

slip knot

Lesson 4: Single Crochet (abbreviated sc)

Our socks are made with variations of just three different stitches: single crochet, double crochet, and half double crochet. The stitches differ mainly in height, which is varied by the number of times the thread is wrapped around the hook. The shortest and most basic of these stitches is the single crochet.

Working Row 1

To practice, begin with the chain of 6 stitches made in Lesson 3 and work the first row of single crochet as follows:

Step 1: Skip first chain stitch from hook. Insert hook in the 2nd chain stitch through the center of the V and under the back bump; with third finger of your left hand, bring yarn over the hook from back to front, and hook the yarn (**Fig 20**).

Fig 20

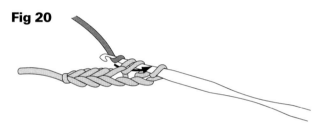

Draw yarn through the chain stitch and well up onto the working area of the hook. You now have 2 loops on the hook (**Fig 21**).

Fig 21

Step 2: Again bring yarn over the hook from back to front, hook it and draw it through both loops on the hook (**Fig 22**).

Fig 22

continued

One loop will remain on the hook, and you have made one single crochet (**Fig 23**).

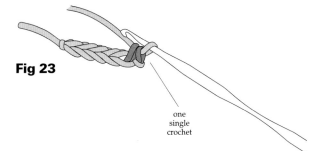

Fig 23

one single crochet

Step 3: Insert hook in next chain stitch as before, hook the yarn, and draw it through the chain stitch; hook yarn again and draw it through both loops: you have made another single crochet.

Repeat Step 3 in each remaining chain stitch, taking care to work in the last chain stitch, but not in the slip knot. You have completed one row of single crochet, and should have 5 stitches in the row. **Fig 24** shows how to count the stitches.

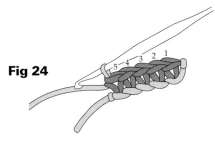

Fig 24

Hint: As you work, be careful not to twist the chain; keep all the Vs facing you.

Working Row 2

To work the second row of single crochet, you need to bring the yarn up to the correct height to work the first stitch, and then turn the work so you can work back across the first row. So to raise the yarn, chain 1 (this is called a turning chain), and then turn the work in the direction of the arrow (counterclockwise) as shown in **Fig 25**.

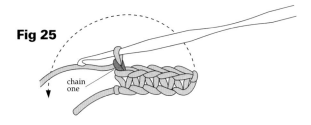

Fig 25

chain one

Do not remove the hook from the loop as you do this (**Fig 25a**).

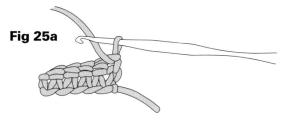

Fig 25a

This row, and all the following rows of single crochet, will be worked into a previous row of single crochet, not into the beginning chain as you did before. Remember that when you worked into the starting chain, you inserted the hook through the center of the V, and under the bump. This is only done when working into a starting chain.

To work into a previous row of crochet, insert the hook under both loops of the previous stitch, as shown in **Fig 26**, instead of through the center of the V.

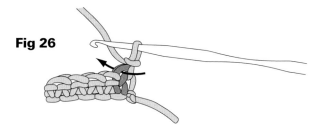

Fig 26

The first single crochet of the row is worked in the last stitch of the previous row (**Fig 26**), not into the turning chain. Work a single crochet in each single crochet to the end, taking care to work in each stitch, especially the last stitch, which is easy to miss (**Fig 27**).

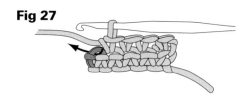

Fig 27

Stop now and count your stitches; you should still have 5 single crochets on the row (**Fig 28**).

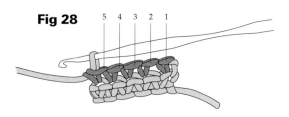

Fig 28

Hint: When you want to pause to count stitches, check your work, have a snack or chat on the phone, you can remove your hook from the work — but do this at the end of a row, not in the middle. To remove the hook, pull straight up on the hook to make a long loop (**Fig 29**).

Fig 29

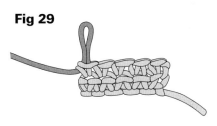

To begin work again, just insert the hook in the big loop (don't twist the loop), and pull on the yarn from the ball to tighten the loop.

To end Row 2, after the last single crochet, chain 1 for the turning chain, and turn the work counterclockwise.

Here is the way instructions for Row 2 might be written in a pattern:

Row 2: Sc in each sc. Ch 1, turn.

Note: To save space, a number of abbreviations and symbols are used. For a list of abbreviations and symbols used in patterns, see page 1.

For practice, work 3 more rows, repeating Row 2.

Finishing Off

It's time to move on to another stitch, so let's finish off your single crochet practice piece, which you can keep for future reference. After the last stitch of the last row, cut the yarn, leaving a 6" end. As you did when you took your hook out for a break, draw the hook straight up, but this time draw the cut end completely through the stitch.

Now you can put the piece away, and it won't pull out (you might want to tag this piece as a sample of single crochet).

Lesson 5: Double Crochet (abbreviated dc)

Double crochet is a taller stitch than single crochet. To practice, first chain 14 stitches loosely. Then work the first row of double crochet as follows:

Working Row 1

Step 1: Bring yarn once over the hook from back to front (as though you were going to make another chain stitch); skip the first three chains from the hook, then insert hook in the 4th chain (**Fig 30**).

Fig 30

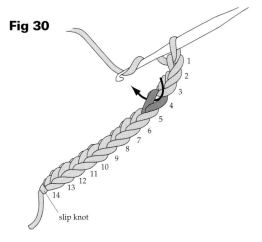

slip knot

Remember not to count the loop on the hook as a chain. Be sure to go through the center of the V of the chain, and under the bump at the back, and not to twist the chain.

Step 2: Hook yarn and draw it through the chain stitch and up onto the working area of the hook. You now have 3 loops on the hook (**Fig 31**).

Fig 31

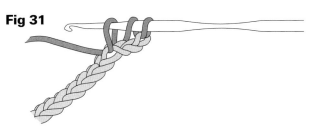

Step 3: Hook yarn and draw through the first 2 loops on the hook (**Fig 32**).

Fig 32

continued

You now have 2 loops on the hook (**Fig 33**).

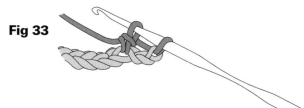

Fig 33

Step 4: Hook yarn and draw through both loops on the hook (**Fig 34**).

Fig 34

You have now completed one double crochet and one loop remains on the hook (**Fig 35**).

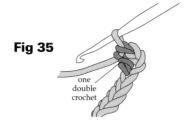

Fig 35

one double crochet

Repeat Steps 1 through 4 in each chain stitch across (except in Step 1, work in next chain, don't skip 3 chains).

When you've worked a double crochet in the last chain, pull out your hook and look at your work, then count your double crochet stitches: there should be 12 of them, counting the first 3 chain stitches you skipped at the beginning of the row as a double crochet (**Fig 36**).

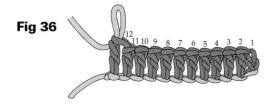

Fig 36

12 11 10 9 8 7 6 5 4 3 2 1

Hint: In working double crochet on a beginning chain row, the 3 chains skipped before making the first double crochet are always counted as a double crochet stitch.

You need to bring the yarn up to the correct height for the next row, and then turn the work. So to raise the yarn, chain 3 (this is called the turning chain); then turn the work counterclockwise before beginning Row 2.

Working Row 2
The 3 chains in the turning chain just made count as the first double crochet of the new row, so skip the first double crochet and work a double crochet in the 2nd stitch (being sure to insert hook under top 2 loops of stitch): **Fig 37** indicates the right and wrong placement of this stitch.

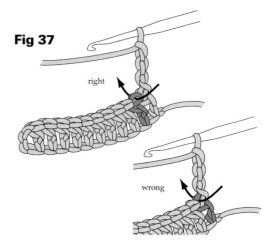

Fig 37

right

wrong

Work a double crochet in each remaining stitch across previous row, and be sure at the end of the row to work the last double crochet in the top of the turning chain from the previous row. Be sure to insert hook in the center of the V (and back bump) of the top chain of the turning chain (**Fig 38**). Stop and count your double crochets; there should be 12 stitches. Now, chain 3 and turn.

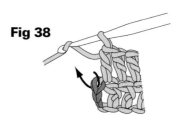

Fig 38

Here is the way the instructions might be written in a regular crochet pattern:

Row 2: Dc in each dc—12 dc. Ch 3, turn.

For practice, work 3 more rows, repeating Row 2. At the end of the last row, do not ch 3. Finish off.

Lesson 6: Half Double Crochet (abbreviated hdc)

Just as its name implies, this stitch eliminates one step of double crochet, and works up about half as tall.

To practice, chain 13 stitches loosely.

Working Row 1

Step 1: Bring yarn once over hook from back to front, skip the first 2 chains, then insert hook in the third chain from the hook (**Fig 39**).

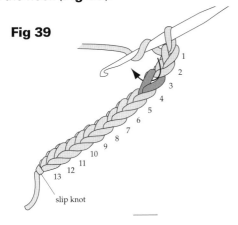

Fig 39

Remember not to count the loop on the hook as a chain.

Step 2: Hook yarn and draw it through the chain stitch and up onto the working area of the hook. You now have 3 loops on the hook (**Fig 40**).

Fig 40

Step 3: Hook yarn and draw it through all 3 loops on the hook in one motion (**Fig 41**).

Fig 41

You have completed one half double crochet and one loop remains on the hook (**Fig 42**).

Fig 42 one half double crochet

In next chain stitch work a half double crochet as follows:

Step 1: Bring yarn once over hook from back to front, insert hook in next chain.

Repeat Steps 2 and 3 of Row 1.

Repeat the previous 3 steps in each remaining chain stitch across. Stop and count your stitches; you should have 12 half double crochets, counting the first 2 chains you skipped at the beginning of the row as a half double crochet (**Fig 43**).

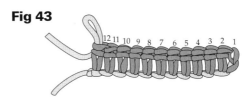

Fig 43

Chain 2 and turn.

Working Row 2

Like double crochet, the turning chain does count as a stitch in half double crochet (unless your pattern specifies otherwise). Skip the first half double crochet of the previous row and work a half double crochet in the second stitch (**Fig 44**) and in each remaining stitch

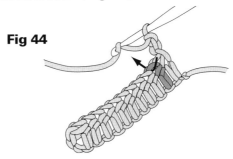

Fig 44

across the previous row. At the end of the row, chain 2 and turn.

Here is the way the instructions might be written in a pattern:

Row 2: Hdc in each hdc—12 hdc. Ch 2, turn.

For practice, work 3 more rows, repeating Row 2. At end of last row, do not ch 3. Finish off.

Lesson 7: Slip Stitch (abbreviated sl st)

This is the shortest of all crochet stitches, and is really more a technique than a stitch. Slip stitches are usually used to move thread across a group of stitches without adding height.

Working Row 1
Chain 10.

Double crochet in the 4th chain from hook (see page 9) and in each chain across. On the next row, you are going to slip stitch across the first four stitches before beginning to work double crochet again. So instead of making 3 chains for the turning chain as you would usually do for a second row of double crochet, this time just chain 1 and turn.

Working Row 2
The turning ch-1 does not count as a stitch; therefore insert hook under both loops of first stitch, hook yarn, and draw it through both loops of stitch and loop on the hook (**Fig 45**): one slip stitch made.

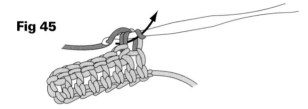

Fig 45

Work a slip stitch in the same manner in each of the next 2 stitches. Now we're going to finish the row in double crochet; chain 3 to get yarn at the right height (the chain 3 counts as a double crochet), then work a double crochet in each of the remaining stitches. Look at your work and see how we moved the thread across with slip stitches, adding very little height (**Fig 46**).

Fig 46

Finish off and save the sample.

Here is the way the instructions might be written in a pattern.

Row 2: Sl st in next 3 dc; ch 3, dc in each dc—5 dc. Finish off.

Hint: When slip stitching across stitches, always work very loosely.

Lesson 8: Pattern Stitches

A pattern stitch is a group of two or more crochet stitches which form a pattern. Instructions for a pattern stitch are either given before the project instructions begin or included as part of the instructions.

Picot
Picots are little loops most often worked in the last round of a project to add a finished look. Picots are made by chaining a specified number of chains, then working a slip stitch into the last stitch worked. Here is the way the instructions might be written in a pattern:

ch 3, sl st in last st made—picot made (**Fig 47**).

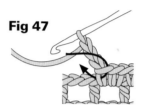

Fig 47

Increasing and Decreasing

Shaping is done by increasing, which adds stitches to make the crocheted piece wider; or decreasing, which subtracts stitches to make the piece narrower.

Note: Make a practice sample by chaining 15 loosely and working 4 rows of single crochet with 14 stitches in each row. Do not finish off at end of last row. Use this sample swatch to practice the following method of increasing stitches.

Increasing: To increase one stitch in single, half double, or double crochet, simply work two stitches in one stitch. For example, if you are working in single crochet and you need to increase one stitch, you would work one single crochet in the next stitch; then you would work another single crochet in the same stitch.

For practice: On sample swatch, chain 1 and turn. Single crochet in first 2 stitches; increase in next stitch by working 2 single crochets in stitch (**Fig 48**).

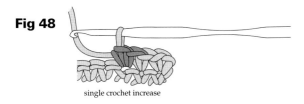

Fig 48

single crochet increase

Repeat increase in each stitch across row to last 2 stitches; single crochet in each of next 2 stitches. Count your stitches; you should have 24 stitches. If you don't have 24 stitches, examine your swatch to see if you have increased in each specified stitch. Rework the row if necessary.

Increases in half double crochet, and double crochet are shown in **Fig 48a**.

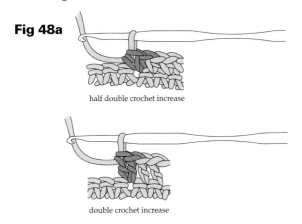

Fig 48a

half double crochet increase

double crochet increase

Note: Make another practice sample by chaining 15 loosely and working 4 rows of single crochet. Do not finish off at end of last row. Use this sample swatch to practice the following methods of decreasing stitches.

Decreasing: This is how to work a decrease in the three main stitches. Each decrease gives one fewer stitch than you had before.

Single Crochet Decrease: Insert hook and draw up a loop in each of the next 2 stitches (3 loops now on hook), hook yarn and draw through all 3 loops on the hook (**Fig 49**).

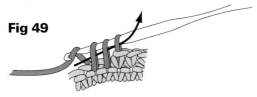

Fig 49

Single crochet decrease made (**Fig 50**).

Fig 50

Double Crochet Decrease: Work a double crochet in the specified stitch until 2 loops remain on the hook (**Fig 51**).

Fig 51

Keeping these 2 loops on hook, work another double crochet in the next stitch until 3 loops remain on hook; hook yarn and draw through all 3 loops on the hook (**Fig 52**).

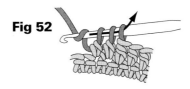

Fig 52

Double crochet decrease made (**Fig 53**).

Fig 53

continued

Special Helps *(continued)*

Joining New Thread

Never tie or leave knots! In crochet, ends can be easily worked in and hidden because of the density of the stitches. Always leave at least 6" ends when finishing off yarn just used and when joining new yarn. If a flaw or a knot appears in the yarn while you are working from a ball, cut out the imperfection and rejoin the yarn.

Whenever possible, join new yarn at the end of a row. To do this, work the last stitch with the old yarn until 2 loops remain on the hook, then with the new yarn complete the stitch (**Fig 54**).

Fig 54

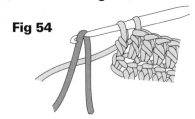

Finishing

A carefully crocheted project can be disappointing if the finishing has been done incorrectly. Correct finishing techniques are not difficult, but do require time, attention, and a knowledge of basic techniques.

Weaving in Ends: The first procedure of finishing is to securely weave in all yarn ends. Thread a size 16 tapestry needle with yarn, then weave running stitches either horizontally or vertically on the wrong side of work. First weave about 1" in one direction and then $\frac{1}{2}$" in the reverse direction. Be sure yarn doesn't show on right side of work and is kept as flat as possible. Cut off excess thread. Never weave in more than one thread end at a time.

Making a Gauge Swatch

If you don't work to gauge, your crocheted socks may not be the correct size, and you may not have enough yarn to finish your project.

Gauge means the number of stitches per inch, that result from a specified yarn worked with a specified size hook. Since everyone crochets differently–some loosely, some tightly, some in between–the measurements of individual work can vary greatly when using the same size hook and yarn. It is your responsibility to make sure you achieve the gauge specified in the pattern.

Hook sizes given in instructions are merely guides and should never be used without making a 4" x 4" sample swatch to check gauge. Make the sample gauge swatch using the size hook, yarn and stitch specified in the pattern. Measure the swatch. If the number of stitches are fewer than indicated under "Gauge" in the pattern, your hook is too large. Try another swatch with a smaller size hook. If the number of stitches are more than indicated under "Gauge" in the pattern, your hook is too small. Try another swatch with a larger size hook. Do not hesitate to change to a larger or smaller size hook if necessary to achieve gauge.

Photo A shows how to measure your gauge.

Photo A

Basic Sock in worsted weight yarn

Size:

	Small	Medium
To Fit Women's Shoe Size	6 to 8	8½ to 10½

Note: Instructions are written for size small; changes for larger size are in parentheses. You may wish to mark all the numbers that apply to the size you are making before beginning.

Materials (sufficient for larger size):

Worsted weight yarn, 3 oz (210 yds, 90 gms) lavender and 2½ (175 yds, 75 gms) pink

Note: Our photographed socks were made with Red Heart® Soft, Lt Amethyst #7582 and Med Rose #7773.
Size H (5mm) crochet hook, or size required for gauge
Safety pins (optional) for markers
Size 16 tapestry needle

Gauge:

4 sc = 1"

Instructions

Sock (make 2)

Cuff:

Note: Cuff is worked vertically in rows.

Starting at center back with lavender, ch 32.

Hint: For ease in identifying right side of work, mark Row 1 with safety pin or contrasting color of yarn.

Row 1 (right side**):**
Sc in 2nd ch from hook and in each rem ch—31 sc. Ch 1, turn.

Row 2:
Working in BLs only (see Terms on page 1), sc in each sc. Ch 1, turn.

Rows 3 through 34 (38):

Rep Row 2. At end of Row 34 (38), do not ch 1. Finish off.

Note: Working in BLs only creates ridges, each two rows worked creates one ridge. When you have completed the 34 (38) rows you will have 17 (19) ridges.

Ankle:

Hold cuff with right side facing you and last row worked to right; with rose make slip knot on hook and join with an sc in edge sc in upper right-hand corner.

Rnd 1 (right side):

Working across cuff in ends of rows, sc in each rem row; sc in joining sc to form a ring (mark this sc with safety pin for beg of rnd)—34 (38) sc **(Photo A)**.

Photo A

Note: The remainder of the ankle is worked in continuous rounds to avoid the bulk of a seam. When working in continuous rounds you do not join at the end of each round but continue working around. It is necessary to mark the first stitch of the round so you know where the round begins. The best way to do this is with a small safety pin in the top of the stitch. The safety pin is moved on each round as you come to it.

Rnd 2:

Sc in each sc.

Rep Rnd 2 until piece measures 2" (2½") from beg of ankle, ending at marker. At end of last rnd, finish off.

Note: Now you will divide piece and work only on heel flap. Because the beginning of the round moves when working continuous rounds, it is necessary to re-position the beginning of the round so the heel is over the seam of the cuff. This means the next round begins to the **right** of beginning marker.

continued

Basic Sock *(continued)*

Heel Flap:

Hold piece with right side facing you and last rnd worked at top; with lavender make slip knot on hook and join with an sc in 6th (7th) sc to **right** of marker.

Row 1 (right side):
Sc in next 16 (18) sc—17 (19) sc. Ch 1, turn, leaving rem 17 (19) sc unworked for instep.

Row 2:
Sc in each sc. Ch 1, turn.

Rows 3 through 8 (10):
Rep Row 2.

Heel Turning:

Row 1 (right side**):**
Sc in next 10 (11) sc. Ch 1, turn, leaving rem 7 (8) sc unworked.

Row 2:
Sc in next 3 sc. Ch 1, turn, leaving rem 7 (8) sc unworked.

Note: Decreases are used on the following rows to shape the heel. They are worked over the next sc on the working row and next unworked sc on heel flap.

Row 3:
Sc in next 2 sc, dec over next sc and next sc on Row 8 (10) [to work dec: draw up lp in next sc on working row and in next unworked sc on row indicated; YO and draw through all 3 lps on hook (see **Fig 1**)—dec made]; sc in next sc on Row 8 (10)—4 sc. Ch 1, turn, leaving 5 (6) unworked sc on Row 8 (10).

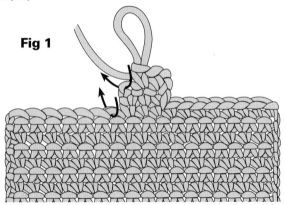

Fig 1

Row 4:
Sc in next 3 sc, dec over next sc and next sc on Row 1, (see **Fig 2**) sc in next sc on Row 1—5 sc. Ch 1, turn, leaving 5 (6) unworked sc on Row 1.

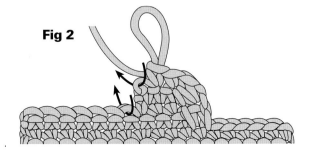

Fig 2

Row 5:
Sc in next 4 sc, dec over next sc and next sc on Row 8 (10); sc in next sc on Row 8 (10)—6 sc. Ch 1, turn, leaving 3 (4) unworked sc on Row 8 (10).

Row 6:
Sc in next 5 sc, dec over next sc and next sc on Row 1; sc in next sc on Row 1—7 sc. Ch 1, turn, leaving 3 (4) unworked sc on Row 1.

Row 7:
Sc in next 6 sc, dec over next sc and next sc on Row 8 (10); sc in next sc on Row 8 (10)—8 sc. Ch 1, turn, leaving 1 (2) unworked sc on Row 8 (10).

Row 8:
Sc in next 7 sc, dec over next sc and next sc on Row 1; sc in next sc on Row 1—9 sc. Ch 1, turn, leaving 1 (2) unworked sc on Row 1.

Note: You can start to see the heel cup forming.

FOR SIZE SMALL ONLY:

Row 9:
Sc in next 9 sc, sc in next sc on Row 8—10 sc. Ch 1, turn.

Row 10:
Sc in next 10 sc, sc in next sc on Row 1—11 sc. Finish off.

Continue with Gusset and Foot below.

FOR SIZE MEDIUM ONLY:

Row 9:
Sc in next 8 sc, dec over next sc and next sc on Row 10, sc in next sc on Row 10—10 sc. Ch 1, turn.

Row 10:
Sc in next 9 sc, dec over next sc and next sc on Row 1, sc in next sc on Row 1—11 sc. Finish off.

Continue with Gusset and Foot.

Gusset and Foot:

Hold piece with right side of heel and cuff seam facing you and last row worked at top; with rose make slip knot on hook and join with an sc in 6th sc of Row 10 of Heel.

Note: Now work in continuous rnds again. Do not join, mark beg of rnds.

Rnd 1:
Sc in next 5 sc, working along side of heel flap in ends of rows, work 9 sc evenly spaced (see Terms on page 1) to last row of flap; dec over next row and first st of instep (mark this st for gusset); sc in next 15 (17) sc, dec over next sc and first row of heel flap (mark this st for gusset); working along side of heel flap in ends of rows, work 9 sc evenly spaced along other side of heel flap, sc in next 5 sc of Row 10 of heel—46 (48) sc.

Note: Now work in continuous rnds again, mark first sc of next rnd for beg of rnd.

Rnd 2:
Sc in each sc to sc before first gusset marker, dec over next sc and marked st (mark this st); sc in next 15 (17) sc, dec over next marked gusset st and next sc (mark this st); sc in each sc to beg marker—44 (46).

Rnds 3 through 7:
Rep Rnd 2. At end of Rnd 7—34 (36) sts.

Note: When working Rnd 8 remove gusset markers. Continue to mark beg of rnd.

Rnd 8:
Sc in each sc.

Rep Rnd 8 until piece measures 2¹/₂" less than desired length of sock (see Guide to Shoe Sizes on page 2). At end of last rnd, finish off. **(Photo B)**

Photo B

Toe Shaping:
Fold sock flat having heel centered in bottom of foot **(Photo C)**. Mark st on each side of foot. You should have 16 (18) sc between each marker. With lavender make slip knot on hook and join with an sc in 9th (10th) st from right marker on bottom of foot (mark for beg of rnd).

Photo C

Note: Toe is worked in continuous rnds. Do not join, mark beg of rnds.

Rnd 1 (right side):
* Sc in each sc to 2 sc before marked side sc, dec over next 2 sc; sc in next sc (mark sc just made), dec over next 2 sc; rep from * once more; sc to beg marker—30 (32) sc.

Rnd 2:
Sc in each sc.

Rnds 3 through 6:
Rep Rnds 1 and 2 twice more. At end of Rnd 6—22 (24) sc.

Rnd 7:
* Sc in each sc to 2 sc before next marked sc, dec over next 2 sc; sc in next sc (mark sc just made), dec over next 2 sc; rep from * once more—18 (20) sc.

Rnds 8 and 9:
Rep Rnd 7. At end of Rnd 9—10 (12) sc. Finish off, leaving a 12" end for sewing.

Finishing
Step 1:
Thread tapestry needle with long end. Turn sock inside out and sew toe being careful to keep seam as flat as possible.

Step 2:
Sew cuff seam together. Weave in all ends.

Basic Sock in sport weight yarn

Size:

	Small	Medium
To Fit Women's Shoe Size	6 to 8	8½ to 10½

Note: Instructions are written for size small; changes for larger size are in parentheses. You may wish to mark all the numbers that apply to the size you are making before begining.

Materials (sufficient for larger size):

Sport weight yarn, 3 oz (270 yds, 90 gms) each blue and variegated

Note: Our photographed socks were made with Patons Look at Me!, Peacock #6360 and Happy Days variegated #6376.

Size E (3.5mm) crochet hook, or size required for gauge

Safety pins (optional) for markers

Size 16 tapestry needle

Gauge:

5 sc = 1"

Instructions

Sock (make 2)

Cuff:

Note: Cuff is worked vertically in rows.

Starting at center back with blue, ch 46.

Hint: For ease in identifying right side, mark Row 1 with a safety pin or contrasting color of yarn.

Row 1 (right side):
Sc in 2nd ch from hook and in each rem ch—45 sc. Ch 1, turn.

Row 2:
Working in BLs only (see Terms on page 1), sc in each sc. Ch 1, turn.

Rows 3 through 42 (46):
Rep Row 2. At end of Row 42 (46) do not ch 1. Finish off.

Note: Working in BLs only creates ridges, each 2 rows worked forms one ridge. When you have completed the 42 (46) rows, you will have 21 (23) ridges.

Ankle:

Hold cuff with right side facing you and last row worked to right; with variegated make lp on hook and join with an sc in edge sc in upper right-hand corner.

Rnd 1 (right side):
Working across cuff in ends of rows, sc in each rem row; sc in joining sc forming a ring (mark this sc with safety pin for beg of rnd)—42 (46) sc. (See **Photo A** on page 15)

Note: The remainder of the ankle is worked in continuous rounds to avoid the bulk of a seam. When working in continuous rounds you do not join at the end of each round, but continue working aorund. It is necessary to mark the first stitch of the round so you know where the round begins. The best way to do this is with a small safety pin in the top of the stitch. The safety pin is moved on each round as you come to it.

Rnd 2:
Sc in each sc.

Rep Rnd 2 until piece measures 2" (2½") from beg of ankle, ending at marker. At end of last rnd, finish off.

Note: Now you will divide piece and work only on heel flap. Because the beginning of the round moves when working in continuous rounds, it is necessary to re-position the beginning of the round, so the heel is over the seam of the cuff. This means the next round begins to the right of the beginning marker.

Heel Flap:

Hold piece with right side facing you and last rnd worked at top, with blue make slip knot on hook and join with an sc in 8th (9th) sc to **right** of marker.

Row 1 (right side):
Sc in next 20 (22) sc—21 (23) sc. Ch 1, turn, leaving rem 21 (23) sc unworked for instep. Remove marker.

Row 2:
Sc in each sc. Ch 1, turn.

Rows 3 through 10:
Rep Row 2.

Heel Turning:

Row 1 (right side):
Sc in next 13 (14) sc. Ch 1, turn, leaving rem 8 (9) sc unworked.

Row 2:
Sc in next 5 sc. Ch 1, turn, leaving rem 8 (9) sc unworked.

Note: Decreases are used on the following rows to shape the heel. They are worked over the next sc on the working row and next unworked sc on heel flap.

Row 3:
Sc in next 4 sc, dec over next sc and next sc on Row 10 [to work dec: draw up lp in next sc on working row and next unworked sc on row indicated; YO and draw through all 3 lps on hook (see **Fig 1**)—dec made]; sc in next sc on Row 10—6 sc. Ch 1, turn, leaving 6 (7) sc unworked on Row 10.

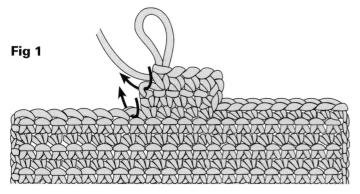

Fig 1

Row 4:
Sc in next 5 sc, dec over next sc on working row and next unworked sc on Row 1, sc in next sc on Row 1—7 sc. Ch 1, turn, leaving 6 (7) sc unworked on Row 1 (see **Fig 2**).

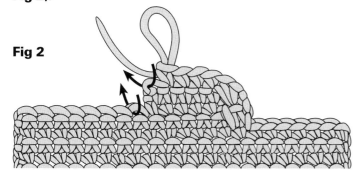

Fig 2

Row 5:
Sc in next 6 sc, dec over next sc and next sc on Row 10; sc in next sc on Row 10—8 sc. Ch 1, turn, leaving 4 (5) sc unworked on Row 10.

Row 6:
Sc in next 7 sc, dec over next sc and next sc on Row 1; sc in next sc on Row 1—9 sc. Ch 1, turn, leaving 4 (5) sc unworked on Row 1.

Row 7:
Sc in next 8 sc, dec over next sc and next sc on Row 10; sc in next sc on Row 10—10 sc. Ch 1, turn, leaving 2 (3) sc unworked on Row 10.

Row 8:
Sc in next 9 sc, dec over next sc and next sc on Row 1; sc in next sc on Row 1—11 sc. Ch 1, turn, leaving 2 (3) sc unworked on Row 1.

Note: You can start to see the heel cup forming.

FOR SIZE SMALL ONLY:
Row 9:
Sc in next 10 sc, dec over next sc on working row and next sc on Row 10—11 sc. Ch 1, turn, leaving rem sc on Row 10 unworked.

Row 10:
Sc in next 10 sc, dec over next sc on working row and next sc on Row 1—11 sc. Ch 1, turn, leaving rem sc on Row 1 unworked.

Row 11:
Sc in next 10 sc, dec over next sc on working row and next sc on Row 10—11 sc. Ch 1, turn.

Row 12:
Sc in next 10 sc, dec over next sc on working row and next sc on Row 1—11 sc. Finish off.

Continue with Gusset and Foot below.

FOR SIZE MEDIUM ONLY:
Row 9:
Sc in next 10 sc, dec over next sc on working row and next sc on Row 10; sc in next sc on Row 10—12 sc. Ch 1, turn, leaving rem sc on Row 10 unworked.

Row 10:
Sc in next 11 sc, dec over next sc on working row and next sc on Row 1; sc in next sc on Row 1—13 sc. Ch 1, turn, leaving rem sc on Row 1 unworked.

Row 11:
Sc in next 12 sc, dec over next sc on working row and next sc on Row 10—13 sc. Ch 1, turn.

Row 12:
Sc in next 12 sc, dec over next sc on working row and next sc on Row 1—13 sc. Finish off.

Continue with Gusset and Foot.

Gusset and Foot:
Note: Now you will begin to work in continuous rnds again; do not join, mark beg of rnds.

Hold piece with right side of heel and cuff seam facing you and last row worked at top; with variegated make slip knot on hook and join with an sc in 6th (7th) sc of Row 12 of Heel.

continued

Basic Sock (continued)

Rnd 1 (right side):
Sc in next 5 (6) sc, working along side of heel flap in ends of rows, work 11 sc evenly spaced (see Terms on page 1) to last row of flap; dec over next row and first st of instep (mark this st for gusset); sc in next 19 (21) sc, dec over next sc and edge sc of first row of heel flap (mark this st for gusset); working along side of heel flap in ends of rows, work 11 sc evenly spaced along other side of heel flap, sc in rem 5 (6) sc of Row 12 of heel—54 (58) sc.

Note: Now work in continuous rnds again, mark first sc of next rnd for beg of rnd.

Rnd 2:
Sc in each sc to sc before first gusset marker, dec over next sc and marked st (mark this st); sc in next 19 (21) sc, dec over next marked gusset st and next sc (mark this st); sc in each sc to beg marker—52 (56) sc.

Rnd 3:
Sc in each sc to st before gusset marker, dec over next sc and marked st (mark this st); sc in next 19 (21) sc, dec over marked st and next sc (mark this st); sc in each sc to beg marker—50 (54) sc.

Rnds 4 through 7:
Rep Rnd 3. At end of Rnd 7—42 (46) sts.

Note: When working Rnd 8 remove gusset markers. Continue to mark beg of rnd.

Rnd 8:
Sc in each sc.

Rep Rnd 8 until piece measures 2¹/₂" less than desired length from beg of heel. At end of last rnd, finish off (see **Photo B** on page 17). Remove marker at beg of rnd.

Toe Shaping:
Fold sock flat having heel centered in bottom of foot (see **Photo C** on page 17). Mark st on each side of foot. You should have 20 (22) sc between each marker. With blue make skip knot on hook and join with an sc in 10th (12th) sc from right marker on bottom of foot (mark for beg of rnd).

Note: Toe is worked in continuous rnds. Do not join, mark beg of rnds.

Rnd 1 (right side):
* Sc in each sc to 2 sc before marked side sc, dec over next 2 sc; sc in next sc (mark sc just made), dec over next 2 sc; rep from * once more; sc to beg marker—38 (42) sc.

Rnd 2:
Sc in each sc.

Rnds 3 through 6:
Rep Rnds 1 and 2 twice more. At end of Rnd 6—30 (34) sc.

Rnd 7:
* Sc in each sc to 2 sc before marked sc, dec over next 2 sc; sc in next sc (mark last sc made), dec over next 2 sc; rep from * once more—26 (30) sc.

Rnds 8 through 11 (12):
Rep Rnd 7. At end of Rnd 11 (12)—10 sc. Finish off, leaving a 12" end for sewing.

Finishing

Step 1:
Thread tapestry needle with long end. Turn sock inside out and sew toe being careful to keep seam as flat as possible.

Step 2:
Sew cuff seam together. Weave in all ends.

Steppin' in Style

worsted weight sock with lace-edge cuff

Size:

	Small	Medium
To Fit Women's Shoe Size	6 to 8	8½ to 10½

Note: Instructions are written for size small; changes for larger size are in parentheses.

Materials (sufficient for larger size):

Worsted weight yarn; 3½ oz (245 yds, 105 gms) variegated and 2½ oz (175 yds, 75 gms) blue

Note: Our photographed socks were made with Red Heart® Soft, Nursery #7965 and Country Blue #7883.

Size H (5mm) crochet hook, or size required for gauge

Safety pins (optional) for markers

Size 16 tapestry needle

Gauge:

4 sc = 1"

Instructions

Sock (make 2)

Cuff:

Note: Cuff is worked vertically in rows.

Starting at center back with variegated, ch 32.

Rows 1 through 34 (38):

Work same as Rows 1 through 34 (38) of Basic Sock Cuff on page 15.

Ankle:

With blue, work same as Basic Sock Ankle on page 15.

Heel Flap and Heel Turning:

With variegated work same as Basic Sock Heel Flap and Heel Turning on page 16.

Gusset and Foot:

With blue, work same as Basic Sock Gusset and Foot beginning on page 16.

Toe Shaping and Finishing:

With variegated, work same as Basic Sock Toe Shaping and Finishing on page 17.

Cuff Edging:

Hold cuff with wrong side facing you; with variegated, make slip knot on hook and join with an sc in seam.

Rnd 1:

Working in ends of rows of cuff, work 35 sc evenly spaced along edge; join in joining sc—36 sc.

Rnd 2:

Ch 1, sc in same sc as joining and in next 4 sc; in next sc work (sc, ch 4, sc); * sc in next 5 sc, in next sc work (sc, ch 4, sc); rep from * 4 times more; join in first sc.

Rnd 3:

Sl st in next 2 sc, ch 1, sc in same sc as last sl st made; * † ch 2, sk next 3 sc, in next ch-4 sp work (sc, ch 5) 3 times; sc in same sp; ch 2, sk next 3 sc †; sc in next sc; rep from * 4 times more, then rep from † to † once; join in first sc.

Rnd 4:

Sl st in next 2 chs, in next sc, and in next ch-5 sp, ch 1, sc in same sp; * † ch 3, in next ch-5 sp work [sc, ch 3, sl st in sc just made (see page 12)—picot made] 3 times; sc in same sp; ch 3, sc in next ch-5 sp †; sk next sc, sc in next ch-5 sp; rep from * 4 times more, then rep from † to † once; join in first sc.

Finish off and weave in all ends.

Fold cuff down.

21

Citrus Shuffle

sport weight sock with shell cuff

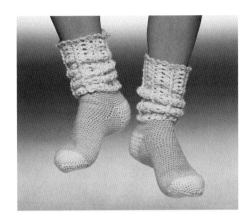

Size:

	Small	Medium
To Fit Women's Shoe Size	6 to 8	8½ to 10½

Note: Instructions are written for size small; changes for larger size are in parentheses.

Materials (sufficient for larger size):

Sport weight yarn, 3 oz (270 yds, 90 gms) each yellow and green

Note: Our photographed socks were made with Patons, Look at Me! Sunny Yellow #6366 and Green Apple #6362.

Size E (3.5mm) crochet hook, or size required for gauge

Safety pins (optional) for markers

Size 16 tapestry needle

Gauge:

5 sc = 1"

Pattern Stitch

Front Post Double Crochet (FPdc):

YO, insert hook from front to back to front around post (see Terms on page 1) of st indicated; (YO, draw through 2 lps on hook) twice—FPdc made.

Instructions

Sock (make 2)

Cuff:

Starting at center back with yellow, ch 42 (48); join to form a ring, being careful not to twist.

Rnd 1 (right side):

Ch 3 (counts as a dc), in same ch work (dc, ch 2, 2 dc)— beg shell made; sk next 2 chs, dc in next ch, sk next 2 chs; * in next ch work (2 dc, ch 2, 2 dc)—shell made; sk next 2 chs, dc in next ch, sk next 2 chs; rep from * 5 (6) times more; join in 3rd ch of beg ch-3—7 (8) shells.

Rnd 2:

Sl st in next dc and in next ch-2 sp, beg shell in same sp; sk next 2 dc of same shell, FPdc (see Pattern Stitch)

around next dc; * in ch-2 sp of next shell work shell; sk next 2 dc of same shell, FPdc around next dc; rep from * 5 (6) times more; join in 3rd ch of beg ch-3.

Rnd 3:

Sl st in next dc and in next ch-2 sp, beg shell in same sp; FPdc around next FPdc; * shell in next shell, FPdc around next FPdc; rep from * 5 (6) times more; join in 3rd ch of beg ch-3.

Rnds 4 through 18:

Rep Rnd 3. At end of Rnd 18, change to green by drawing lp through.

Rnd 19:

Ch 1, in same ch as joining work (sc, ch 3, sc); sk next dc; *† in next ch-2 sp work (sc, ch 3, sc); sk next dc, in next dc work (sc, ch 3, sc); sk next FPdc †; in next dc work (sc, ch 3, sc); sk next dc; rep from * 5 (6) times more, then rep from † to † once; join in first sc. Finish off.

Ankle:

Hold cuff with right side facing you and beg ch at top; with green make slip knot on hook and join with an sc in first unused lp of beg ch.

Rnd 1 (right side):

Working in rem unused lps and skipped chs of beg ch, sc in each st; join in joining sc—42 (48) sc.

Note: Remainder of ankle is worked in continuous rnds; do not join, mark beg of rnds.

Rnd 2 (for size small only):

Sc in each sc.

Rnd 2 (for size medium only):

Dec over next 2 sc (to work dec: draw up lp in each of next 2 sc, YO and draw through all 3 lps on hook—dec made); sc in next 22 sc, dec over next 2 sc; sc in next 22 sc—46 sc.

Rnd 3 (for both sizes):

Sc in each sc.

Rep Rnd 3 until piece measures 1½" from beg of ankle, ending at marker. At end of last rnd, finish off.

Note: Now you will divide piece and work only on heel.

Heel Flap and Heel Turning:

With yellow, work same as Basic Sock Heel Flap and Heel Turning beginning on page 18.

Gusset and Foot:

With green, work same as Basic Sock Gusset and Foot on page 19.

Toe Shaping and Finishing:

With yellow, work same as Basic Sock Toe Shaping and Finishing on page 20.

In the Wild

worsted weight sock with stripe cuff

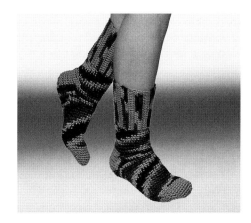

Size:

	Small	Medium
To Fit Women's Shoe Size	6 to 8	$8^1/_2$ to $10^1/_2$

Note: Instructions are written for size small; changes for larger size are in parentheses.

Materials (sufficient for larger size):

Worsted weight yarn, $3^1/_2$ oz (245 yds, 105 gms) variegated and $2^1/_2$ oz (175 yds, 75 gms) green
Note: Our photographed socks were made with Red Heart® Super Saver, Medium Celery #616 and Camouflage #971.
Size H (5mm) crochet hook, or size required for gauge
Safety pins (optional) for markers
Size 16 tapestry needle

Gauge:

4 sc = 1"

Instructions

Sock (make 2)

Cuff:

Note: Cuff is worked vertically in rows. To change colors work until 2 lps of last st remain on hook, with new color draw lp through. On cuff carry old color along edge until needed.

Starting at center back with green, ch 24.

Row 1 (right side):
Sc in 2nd ch from hook and in each rem ch—23 sc. Ch 1, turn.

Row 2:
Working in BLs only, sc in each sc, changing to variegated in last sc. Ch 1, turn.

Row 3:
Working in BLs only, sc in each sc. Ch 1, turn.

Row 4:
Rep Row 3, changing to green in last sc.

Row 5:
Rep Row 3.

Row 6:
Rep Row 3, changing to variegated in last sc.

Rows 7 through 30 (34):
Rep Rows 3 through 6 six (7) times more.

Rows 31 (35) and 32 (36):
Rep Rows 3 and 4. At end of Row 32 (36), do not ch 1. Finish off.

Ankle:

Hold cuff with right side facing you and last row worked to left; with variegated make slip knot on hook and join with an sc in edge sc in upper right-hand corner.

Rnd 1 (right side):
Working across cuff in ends of rows, sc in each rem row—32 (36) sc; sc in joining sc (mark last sc made for beg of rnd).

Note: Remainder of ankle is worked in continuous rnds. Do not join; mark beg of rnds.

Rnd 2:
* Sc in next 10 (11) sc, 2 sc in next sc; rep from * once more; sc in next 10 (12) sc—34 (38) sc.

Rnd 3:
Sc in each sc.
Rep Rnd 3 until piece measures 2" ($2^1/_2$") from beg of ankle, ending at marker. At end of last rnd, finish off.

Heel Flap and Heel Turning:

With green, work same as Basic Sock Heel Flap and Heel Turning beginning on page 16.

Gusset and Foot:

With variegated, work same as Basic Sock Gusset and Foot beginning on page 16.

Toe Shaping and Finishing:

With green, work same as Basic Sock Toe Shaping and Finishing on page 17.

Leapin' Lavender

sport weight sock with lace-edge cuff

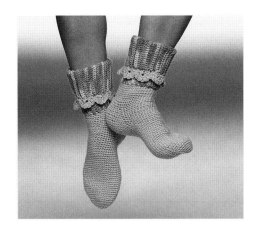

Size:

	Small	Medium
To Fit Women's Shoe Size	6 to 8	$8\frac{1}{2}$ to $10\frac{1}{2}$

Note: Instructions are written for size small; changes for larger size are in parentheses.

Materials (sufficient for larger size):

Sport weight yarn, $3\frac{1}{2}$ oz (315 yds, 105 gms) lavender and $2\frac{1}{2}$ oz (225 yds, 75 gms) variegated

Note: Our photographed socks were made with Patons Look at Me!, Lilac #6358 and Fun 'n Games variegated #6377.

Size E (3.5mm) crochet hook, or size required for gauge
Safety pins (optional) for markers
Size 16 tapestry needle

Gauge:

5 sc = 1"

Instructions

Sock (make 2)

Cuff:

Note: Cuff is worked vertically in rows.

Starting at center back with variegated, ch 38.

Row 1 (right side):
Sc in 2nd ch from hook and in each rem ch—37 sc. Ch 1, turn.

Rows 2 through 42 (46):
Work same as Rows 2 through 42 (46) of Basic Sock Cuff on page 18.

Ankle:
With lavender, work same as Basic Sock Ankle on page 18.

Heel Flap and Heel Turning:
With lavender, work same as Basic Sock Heel Flap and Heel Turning beginning on page 18.

Gusset and Foot:

With lavender, work same as Basic Sock Gusset and Foot beginning on page 19.

Toe Shaping:

With lavender, work same as Basic Sock Toe Shaping on page 20.

Sew cuff seam.

Cuff Trim:

Hold cuff with wrong side facing you and unused edge of rows at top. With lavender make slip knot on hook and join with an sc in cuff seam.

Rnd 1:
Working along edge of cuff in ends of rows, sc in next 41 (45) rows; join in joining sc—42 (46) sc.

Rnd 2 (for size small only):
Ch 1, 2 sc in same sc as joining; sc in next 3 sc, in next sc work (sc, ch 4, sc); sc in next 5 sc, in next sc work (sc, ch 4, sc); † 2 sc in next sc; sc in next 3 sc; in next sc work (sc, ch 4, sc) †; rep from † to † twice more; sc in next 5 sc, in next sc work (sc, ch 4, sc); rep from † to † twice; join in first sc—8 ch-4 sps.

Rnd 2 (for size medium only):
Ch 1, 2 sc in same sc as joining; sc in next 3 sc, in next sc work (sc, ch 4, sc); † dc in next 5 sc, in next sc work (sc, ch 4, sc) †; rep from † to † twice more; 2 sc in next sc; sc in next 3 sc, in next sc work (sc, ch 4, sc); rep from † to † 3 times; join in first sc—8 ch-4 sps.

Rnd 3 (for both sizes):
Sl st in next 2 sc, ch 1, sc in same sc as last sl st made; ch 2, 5 sc in next ch-4 sp; ch 2, sk next 3 sc; * sc in next sc, ch 2, 5 sc in next ch-4 sp; ch 2, sk next 3 sc; rep from * 6 times more; join in first sc.

Rnd 4:
Ch 1, sc in same sc; * † sk next ch-2 sp (sc in next sc, ch 3) 4 times †; sc in next sc, sk next ch-2 sp, sc in next sc; rep from * 6 times more, then rep from † to † once; sc in next sc; join in first sc. Finish off and weave in ends.

Finishing

Thread tapestry needle with long end. Turn sock inside out and sew last rnd of toe.

Mango Tango

sport weight sock with ruffle heel

Size:

	Small	Medium
To Fit Women's Shoe Size	6 to 8	8½ to 10½

Note: Instructions are written for size small; changes for larger size are in parentheses.

Materials (sufficient for larger size):

Sport weight yarn, 5 oz (456 yds, 150 gms) coral and ½ oz (45 yds, 15 gms) white
Note: Our photographed socks were made with Patons Look at Me!, Mango #6356 and White #6351.
Size E (3.5mm) crochet hook, or size required for gauge
Safety pins (optional) for markers
Size 16 tapestry needle

Gauge:

5 sc = 1"

Instructions

Sock (make 2)

Cuff:
Note: Cuff is worked vertically in rows.
Starting at center back with coral, ch 25.

Row 1 (right side):
Sc in 2nd ch from hook and in each rem ch—24 sc. Ch 1, turn.

Rows 2 through 42 (46):
Work same as Rows 2 through 42 (46) of Basic Sock Cuff on page 18.

Ankle:
With coral, work same as Basic Sock Ankle on page 18.

Heel Flap:
Hold piece with right side facing you and last rnd worked at top, with coral make slip knot on hook and join with an sc in 8th (10th) sc to **right** of marker.

Row 1 (right side):
Sc in next 20 (22) sc—21 (23) sc. Ch 1, turn, leaving rem 21 (23) sc unworked for instep. Remove marker.

Row 2:
Working in FLs only (see Terms on page 1), sc in each sc. Ch 1, turn.

Row 3:
Working through both loops, sc in each sc. Ch 1, turn.

Rows 4 through 9:
Rep Rows 2 and 3 three times more.

Row 10:
Rep Row 2.

Heel Turning:
With coral, work same as Basic Sock Heel Turning beginning on page 18.

Gusset and Foot:
With coral, work same as Basic Sock Gusset and Foot beginning on page 19.

Toe Shaping and Finishing:
With coral, work same as Basic Sock Toe Shaping and Finishing on page 20.

Heel Ruffle:
Hold piece with right side and cuff seam facing you. With white make slip knot on hook and join with an sc in first unused lp of Row 1 of Heel Flap; * ch 3, working in rem unused lps of Row 1 of Heel Flap, sc in next lp; rep from * across. Finish off.
Rep Heel Ruffle in unused lps of Rows 3, 5, 7 and 9 of Heel Flap.

Cuff Ruffle:
Hold piece with right side facing you and unworked edge of cuff at top; with white make slip knot on hook and join with an sc in cuff seam; ch 3; working in in ends of rows in edge sc, * sc in next row, ch 3; rep from * around; join in first sc.

Finish off and weave in ends.

Rippled Effect

worsted weight sock with chevron cuff

Size:

	Small	Medium
To Fit Women's Shoe Size	6 to 8	8½ to 10½

Note: Instructions are written for size small; changes for larger size are in parentheses.

Materials (sufficient for larger size):

Worsted weight yarn, 3½ oz (245 yds, 105 gms) black;
    1 oz (70 yds, 30 gms) each pink and blue
Note: Our photographed socks were made with Red Heart® Soft, Black #7012, Med Blue #7821 and Fuchsia #7769.
Size H (5mm) crochet hook, or size required for gauge
Safety pins (optional) for markers
Size 16 tapestry needle

Gauge:

4 sc = 1"

Instructions

Sock (make 2)

Cuff:

With black, ch 44 (55); join to form a ring, being careful not to twist.

Rnd 1 (right side):

Ch 1, sc in same ch and in next 3 chs; 3 sc in next ch; sc in next 4 chs, sk next 2 chs; * sc in next 4 chs, 3 sc in next ch; sc in next 4 chs, sk next 2 chs; rep from * 2 (3) times more; join in BL (see Terms on page 1) of first sc.

Rnd 2:

Sl st in BL of next sc, change to blue by drawing lp through; cut black, ch 1, sc in same lp; working in BLs only, sc in next 3 sc, 3 sc in next sc; sc in next 4 sc, sk next 2 sc; * sc in next 4 sc, 3 sc in next sc; sc in next 4 sc, sk next 2 sc; rep from * 2 (3) times more; join in BL of first sc.

Rnd 3:

Sl st in BL of next sc, ch 1, sc in same lp; working in BLs only, sc in next 3 sc, 3 sc in next sc; sc in next 4 sc, sk next 2 sc; * sc in next 4 sc, 3 sc in next sc; sc in next 4 sc, sk next 2 sc; rep from * 2 (3) times more; join in BL of first sc.

Rnd 4:

Sl st in BL of next sc, change to black by drawing lp through; cut blue, ch 1, sc in same lp; working in BLs only, sc in next 3 sc, 3 sc in next sc; sc in next 4 sc, sk next 2 sc; * sc in next 4 sc, 3 sc in next sc; sc in next 4 sc, sk next 2 sc; rep from * 2 (3) times more; join in BL of first sc.

Rnd 5:

Sl st in BL of next sc, change to pink by drawing lp through; cut black, ch 1, sc in same lp; working in BLs only, sc in next 3 sc, 3 sc in next sc; sc in next 4 sc, sk next 2 sc; * sc in next 4 sc, 3 sc in next sc; sc in next 4 sc, sk next 2 sc; rep from * 2 (3) times more; join in BL of first sc.

Rnd 6:

Rep Rnd 3.

Rnd 7:

Sl st in BL of next sc, change to black by drawing lp through; cut pink, ch 1, sc in same lp; working in BLs only, sc in next 3 sc, 3 sc in next sc; sc in next 4 sc, sk next 2 sc; * sc in next 4 sc, 3 sc in next sc; sc in next 4 sc, sk next 2 sc; rep from * 2 (3) times more; join in BL of first sc.

Rnds 8 through 13:

Rep Rnds 2 through 7.

Rnds 14 and 15:

Rep Rnds 2 and 3.

Rnd 16 (for size small only):

Sl st through both lps of next sc, change to black by drawing lp through; cut blue, ch 1, sc in same lp and in next 8 sc; sk next 2 sc; * sc in next 9 sc, sk next 2 sc; rep from * twice more; join in first sc—36 sc.

Rnd 16 (for size medium only):

Sl st through both lps of next sc, change to black by drawing lp through; cut blue, ch 1, sc in same lp and in next 3 sc; sk next sc, sc in next 4 sc, sk next 2 sc; * sc in next 4 sc, sk next sc, sc in next 4 sc, sk next 2 sc; rep from * 3 times more; join in first sc—40 sc.

Ankle:

Rnd 1 (right side):

Ch 1, sc in same sc and in next 9 (11) sc; dec over next 2 sc (to work dec: draw up lp in each of next 2 sc, YO and draw through all 3 lps on hook—dec made); sc in next 10 (12) sc, dec over next 2 sc; sc in next 12 sc; join in first sc—34 (38) sc.

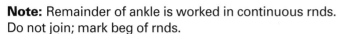

Note: Remainder of ankle is worked in continuous rnds. Do not join; mark beg of rnds.

Rnd 2:
Sc in each sc.

Rep Rnd 2 until piece measures 1¹/₂" **(2")** from beg of ankle, ending at marker. At end of last rnd, finish off.

Note: Now you will divide piece and work only on heel.

Heel Flap and Heel Turning:
With pink, work same as Basic Sock Heel Flap and Heel Turning beginning on page 16.

Gusset and Foot:
With black, work same as Basic Sock Gusset and Foot beginning on page 16.

Toe Shaping and Finishing:
With blue, work same as Basic Sock Toe Shaping and Finishing on page 17.

Primary Hues

sport weight sock with stripe cuff

Size:

	Small	Medium
To Fit Women's Shoe Size	6 to 8	8¹/₂ to 10¹/₂

Note: Instructions are written for size small; changes for larger size are in parentheses.

Materials (sufficient for larger size):
Sport weight yarn, 2¹/₂ oz (225 yds, 75 gms) blue; 1¹/₂ oz (135 yds, 45 gms) each red and green; 1 oz (90 yds, 30 gms) yellow

Note: Our photographed socks were made with Patons Look at Me!, Bright Blue #6367, Racy Red #6365, Kelly Green #6368, and Sunny Yellow #6366.

Size E (3.5mm) crochet hook, or size required for gauge

Safety pins (optional) for markers

Size 16 tapestry needle

Gauge:
5 sc = 1"

Instructions

Sock (make 2)

Cuff:
Note: Cuff is worked vertically in rows. To change colors, work until 2 lps of color remain on hook, with new color, draw through 2 lps on hook. Cut old color.

Starting at center back with blue, ch 41.

Row 1 (right side):
Sc in 2nd ch from hook and in each rem ch—40 sc. Ch 1, turn.

Row 2:
Working in BLs only (see Terms on page 1), sc in each sc, changing to yellow in last sc. Ch 1, turn.

continued

Row 3:
Working in BLs only, sc in each sc. Ch 1, turn.

Row 4:
Rep Row 3, changing to green in last sc.

Rows 5 and 6:
Rep Row 3. At end of Row 6, change to red.

Rows 7 and 8:
Rep Row 3. At end of Row 8, change to blue.

Rows 9 and 10:
Rep Row 3. At end of Row 10, change to yellow.

Rows 11 through 42:
Rep Rows 3 through 10 four times more.

FOR SIZE SMALL ONLY:
At end of Row 42, do not change color, do not ch 1. Finish off.

Continue with Ankle below.

FOR SIZE MEDIUM ONLY:
Rows 43 through 46:
Rep Rows 3 through 6. At end of Row 46, do not change color, do not ch 1. Finish off.

Continue with Ankle.

Ankle:
Hold cuff with wrong side facing you and last row worked to right; with blue make slip knot on hook and join with an sc in edge sc in upper right-hand corner.

Rnd 1:
Working across cuff in ends of rows, sc in each rem row; sc in joining sc forming a ring (mark sc just made for beginning of rnd)—42 (46) sc.

Note: Remainder of ankle is worked in continuous rnds; do not join, mark beg of rnds.

Rnd 2:
Sc in each sc.

Rep Rnd 2 until piece measures 2" (2½") from beg of ankle, ending at marker. At end of last rnd, finish off.

Note: Now you will divide piece and work only on heel.

Heel Flap and Heel Turning:
With red work same as Basic Sock Heel Flap and Heel Turning beginning on page 18.

Gusset and Foot:
With blue, work same as Basic Sock Gusset and Foot begining on page 19.

Toe Shaping and Finishing:
With green, work same as Basic Sock Toe Shaping and Finishing on page 20.

Cuff Trim:
Hold sock with wrong side facing you and unused edge of cuff at top; with yellow make slip knot on hook and join with an sc in cuff seam.

Rnd 1:
Working in edge sc of cuff, work 43 (47) evenly spaced (see Terms on page 1) around; join in joining sc— 44 (48) sc.

Rnd 2:
Ch 1, 3 sc in same sc; ch 2, sk next 3 sc; ✱ 3 sc in next sc; ch 2, sk next 3 sc; rep from ✱ 9 (10) times more; join in first sc.

Rnd 3:
Sl st in next sc, ch 1, in same sc work [sc, ch 3, sl st in sc just made (see page 12)—picot made, sc]; ch 1, sc in next ch-2 sp, ch 1, sk next sc; ✱ in next sc work (sc, ch 3, sl st in sc just made—picot made, sc); ch 1, sc in next ch-2 sp, ch 1; rep from ✱ 9 (10) times more; join in first sc.

Finish off and weave in ends.

Fold cuff down.

Tip-Toe in the Meadow
worsted weight sock with shell-stripe cuff

Size:

	Small	Medium
To Fit Women's Shoe Size	6 to 8	$8\frac{1}{2}$ to $10\frac{1}{2}$

Note: Instructions are written for size small; changes for larger size are in parentheses.

Materials (sufficient for larger size):
Worsted weight yarn; $3\frac{1}{2}$ oz (245 yds, 105 gms) variegated and $2\frac{1}{2}$ oz (175 yds, 75 gms) green
Note: Our photographed socks were made with Red Heart® Soft, Key West #7939 and Emerald #7668.
Size H (5mm) crochet hook, or size required for gauge
Safety pins (optional) for markers
Size 16 tapestry needle

Gauge:
4 sc = 1"

Instructions

Sock (make 2)

Cuff:
Note: Cuff is worked vertically in rows. To change colors in an sc work until 2 lps of last st remain on hook, with new color draw lp through. Cut old color. To change colors in an hdc work until 3 lps of last st remain on hook, with new color draw lp through. Cut old color.
Starting at center back with green, ch 28.

Row 1 (wrong side):
Sc in 2nd ch from hook and in each rem ch—27 sc. Ch 1, turn.

Row 2 (right side):
Working in BLs only (see Terms on page 1), sc in each sc, changing to variegated in last sc; cut green. Ch 2 (counts as an hdc on following rows), turn.

Row 3:
Working in BLs only, hdc in next sc; * † sk next 2 sc, in next sc work (2 hdc, ch 1, 2 hdc); sk next 2 sc †; hdc in next 4 sc; rep from * once more, then rep from † to † once; hdc in next 2 sc, changing to green in last hdc; cut variegated. Ch 1, turn.

Row 4:
Working in BLs only, sc in each hdc, in each ch and in 2nd ch of turning ch-2—27 sc. Ch 1, turn.

Row 5:
Working in BLs only, sc in each sc. Ch 1, turn.

Rows 6 and 7:
Rep Row 5.

Row 8:
Rep Row 2.

Rows 9 through 32:
Rep Rows 3 through 8 four times more.

Rows 33 and 34:
Rep Rows 3 and 4.

FOR SIZE SMALL ONLY:
At end of Row 34, do not ch 1.
Finish off and weave in all ends.
Continue with Ankle below.

FOR SIZE MEDIUM ONLY:
Rows 35 and 36:
Rep Row 5. At end of Row 36, do not ch 1.
Finish off and weave in all ends.
Continue with Ankle.

Ankle:
Hold cuff with right side facing you and last row worked to right; with variegated make slip knot on hook and join with an sc in edge sc of first row in upper right-hand corner.

Rnd 1 (right side):
Working across cuff in edge sc and in sps formed by turning chs and hdc rows, work 33 (35) sc evenly spaced (see Terms on page 1) across; sc in joining sc (mark last sc made for beg of rnd)—34 (36) sc.

Note: Ankle is worked in continuous rnds; do not join, mark beg of rnds.

continued

Tip-Toe in the Meadow (continued)

Rnd 2 (for size small only):
Sc in each sc.

Rnd 2 (for size medium only):
* Sc in next 11 sc, 2 sc in next sc; rep from * once more; sc in next 12 sc—38 sc.

Rnd 3 (for both sizes):
Sc in each sc.
Rep Rnd 3 until piece measures 1½" (2") from beg of ankle, ending at marker. At end of last rnd, finish off.

Heel Flap and Heel Turning:
With green, work same as Basic Sock Heel Flap and Heel Turning beginning on page 16.

Gusset and Foot:
With variegated, work same as Basic Sock Gusset and Foot beginning on page 16.

Toe Shaping and Finishing:
With green, work same as Basic Sock Toe Shaping and Finishing on page 17.

Dancing Crayons
sport weight sock with ripple cuff

Size:

	Small	Medium
To Fit Women's Shoe Size	6 to 8	8½ to 10½

Note: Instructions are written for size small; changes for larger size are in parentheses.

Materials (sufficient for larger size):
Sport weight yarn, 3½ oz (315 yds, 105 gms) variegated;
   1 oz (90 yds, 30 gms) each blue and red
Note: Our photographed sock were made with Jamie®
3 Ply Baby, Circus Print #267, Colonial Blue #209 and
Scarlet #213
Size F (3.75mm) crochet hook, or size required for gauge
Size G (4.25mm) crochet hook
Size 16 tapestry needle (for weaving in ends)

Gauge:
With smaller size hook:
5 sc = 1"

Instructions

Sock (make 2)

Cuff:
Starting at center back with larger size hook and blue, ch 42 (49); join to form a ring being careful not to twist.

Change to smaller size hook.

Row 1 (right side):
Ch 1, sc in same ch as joining and in next ch; 3 sc in next ch; sc in next 2 chs, sk next 2 chs; * sc in next 2 chs, 3 sc in next ch; sc in next 2 chs, sk next 2 chs; rep from * 4 (5) times more; join in BL (see Terms on page 1) of first sc.

Row 2:
Sl st in next sc, ch 1, working in Bls only, sc in same sc and in next sc; 3 sc in next sc; sc in next 2 sc, sk next 2 sc; * sc in next 2 sc, 3 sc in next sc; sc in next 2 sc, sk next 2 sc; rep from * 4 (5) times more; join in BL of first sc, changing to variegated by drawing lp through; cut blue.

Row 3:
Sl st in next sc, ch 1, working in Bls only, sc in same sc and in next sc; 3 sc in next sc; sc in next 2 sc, sk next 2 sc; * sc in next 2 sc, 3 sc in next sc; sc in next 2 sc, sk next 2 sc; rep from * 4 (5) times more; join in BL of first sc.

Rows 4 through 6:
Rep Row 3. At end of Row 6, change to red by drawing lp through; cut variegated.

Rows 7 and 8:
Rep Row 3. At end of Row 8, change to variegated by drawing lp through; cut red.

Rows 9 through 12:
Rep Row 3. At end of Row 12, change to blue by drawing lp through; cut variegated.

Rows 13 and 14:
Rep Row 3. At end of Row 14, change to variegated; cut blue.

Row 15 through 18:
Rep Row 3. At end of Row 18, change to red; cut variegated.

Rows 19 and 20:
Rep Row 3. At end of Row 20, join through both lps of first sc. Finish off.

Ankle:
Hold cuff with right side facing you and beg ch at top; with variegated, make slip knot on smaller size hook and join with an sc in first unused lp of beg ch.

Rnd 1 (right side):
Working in rem unused lps and chs, sc in each lp; join in joining sc—42 (49) sc.

Rnd 2 (for size small only):
Ch 1, sc in each sc; join in first sc—42 sc.

Rnd 2 (for size medium only):
Ch 1, dec over first 2 sc (to work dec: draw up lp in each of next 2 sc, YO and draw through all 3 lps on hook—dec made); sc in next 14 sc, dec over next 2 sc; sc in next 15 sc, dec over next 2 sc; sc in next 14 sc; join in first sc—46 sc.

Note: Remainder of ankle is worked in continuous rnds; do not join, mark beg of rnds.

Rnd 3 (for both sizes):
Sc in each sc.

Rep Rnd 3 until piece measures 2" from beg of ankle, ending at marker. At end of last rnd, finish off.

Note: Now you will divide piece and work only on heel.

Heel Flap and Heel Turning:
With red, work same as Basic Sock Heel Flap and Heel Turning beginning on page 18.

Gusset and Foot:
With variegated, work same as Basic Sock Gusset and Foot beginning on page 19.

Toe Shaping:
With blue, work same as Basic Sock Toe Shaping on page 20.

Finishing
Thread tapestry needle with long end. Turn sock inside out and sew last rnd of toe. Weave in all ends.

Footloose

lacy tube sock

Size:
One size fits most foot and leg measurements.

Materials:
Sport weight yarn, 3½ oz (315 yds, 105 gms) white
Note: Our photographed socks were made with Patons
Look at Me!, White #6351
Size F (3.75mm) crochet hook, or size required for gauge
Size G (4.25 mm) crochet hook
Size H (5mm) crochet hook

Gauge:
With smallest size hook in pattern:
2 shells = 2"

Instructions

Sock (make 2)
Starting at toe, with smallest size hook, ch 2.

Rnd 1 (right side):
In 2nd ch from hook work 8 sc; join in first sc.

Rnd 2:
Ch 1, 2 sc in same sc and in each rem sc; join in first sc—
16 sc.

Rnd 3:
Ch 3 (counts as a dc), 2 dc in next sc; * dc in next sc, 2 dc
in next sc; rep from * 6 times more; join in 3rd ch of beg
ch-3—24 dc.

Rnd 4:
Ch 3, dc in next 4 dc, 2 dc in next dc; * dc in next 5 dc,
2 dc in next dc; rep from * twice more; join in 3rd ch of
beg ch-3—28 dc.

Note: Remainder of sock is worked in continuous rnds.
Do not join, mark beg of rnds.

Rnd 5:
* † Sc in next dc, sk next dc, in next dc work (dc, ch 1, dc,
ch 1, dc)—shell made †; sk next dc; rep from * 5 times
more, then rep from † to † once; sk next sl st and first sc—
7 shells; do not join.

Rnd 6:
* Sc in 2nd dc of next shell, shell in next sc; rep from
* 5 times more; sc in 2nd dc of next shell—6 shells.

Rnd 7:
* Shell in next sc, sc in 2nd dc of next shell; rep from
* 5 times more; shell in next sc—7 shells.

Rnds 8 through 15:
Rep Rnds 6 and 7 four times more.

Change to medium size hook.

Rnds 16 through 25:
Rep Rnds 6 and 7 five times.

Change to largest size hook.

Rnd 26:
* Sc in 2nd dc of next shell, in next sc work (dc, ch 1) 3
times; dc in same sc—4-dc shell made; rep from * 5 times
more; sc in 2nd dc of next shell—six 4-dc shells.

Rnd 27:
* 4-dc shell in next sc; sc in 2nd ch-1 sp of next shell;
rep from * 5 times more; 4-dc shell in next sc—
seven 4-dc shells.

Rnd 28:
* Sc in 2nd ch-1 sp of next shell; 4-dc shell in next sc;
rep from * 5 times more; sc in 2nd ch-1 sp of next shell—
six 4-dc shells.

Rnds 29 through 42:
Rep Rnds 27 and 28 seven times more.

Cuff:
Sl st in next sc, ch 1, sc in same sc, in each dc, in each
ch-1 sp and in each sc around; join in first sc—49 sc.

Finish off and weave in ends.